**mommy's
having
a baby**

Design Pamela Daniels
Commissioning editor Annabel Morgan
Production manager Patricia Harrington
Art director Gabriella Le Grazie
Publishing director Alison Starling

First published in the United States
in 2005 by Ryland Peters & Small, Inc.
519 Broadway, 5th Floor
New York, NY 10012
www.rylandpeters.com

10 9 8 7 6 5 4 3 2

Text, design, and commissioned photographs
© Ryland Peters & Small 2005

ISBN-10: 1-84172-840-3
ISBN-13: 978-1-84172-840-7

Printed in China

**For Christian and Chad,
where the book began.**

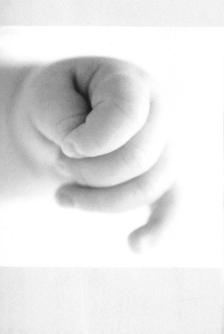

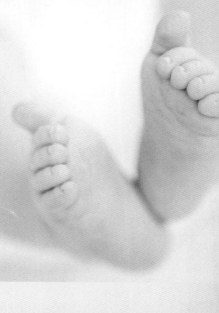

mommy's having a baby

A special book for mommy's first child

CAMILLE LISCINSKY

RYLAND
PETERS
& SMALL
LONDON NEW YORK

place photo
of your
firstborn here

This book is for

_____

with lots of love,

_____

Our family is having a baby.

This book tells about you and the baby.

Mommy will write words in the book.

You can draw pictures in the book.

We can glue pictures, too.

Together we will make a special book

that is just for you.

When you were a baby

draw a picture
of your family
and attach
here

Once upon a time, you were a baby.

A happy day.

_____,
you are Mommy and Daddy's first
child. You made Mommy and Daddy
very happy when you were born!
On the day you were born,
I remember that

_____.

You were born on

_____.

People said, "_____

is a _____ baby!"

A baby is small.

You were as small as a

_____ when you were a baby.

You liked to _____

and _____.

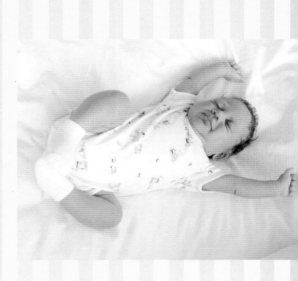

You were this small when you were born.

_____ inches.

Now you are bigger.

You are Mommy's special helper.

You can help Mommy get ready for our baby.

Mommy's having a baby

**One day, we don't know when,
our baby will be born.**

Draw a picture of Mommy.

_____, you can see how big our baby is growing inside of Mommy.

Our baby makes Mommy look different!

Put your hand on Mommy's tummy.

attach
ultrasound
picture here

Is our baby moving or is our baby sleeping?

Our baby is getting ready to be born.

One day Mommy will feel the
baby move into place.

The baby may move while
Mommy is sleeping,

when Mommy's playing with you,

or when Mommy is working.

Anytime!

My Mommy and I like to _____ together.

When the baby moves into place,
Mommy or Daddy will call
Doctor _____ and say,
**"Our baby is ready
to be born!"**

Doctor _____ will say,
**"That's good news!
I will meet you at the hospital."**

Mommy will go to

hospital right away,
even if it's nighttime.

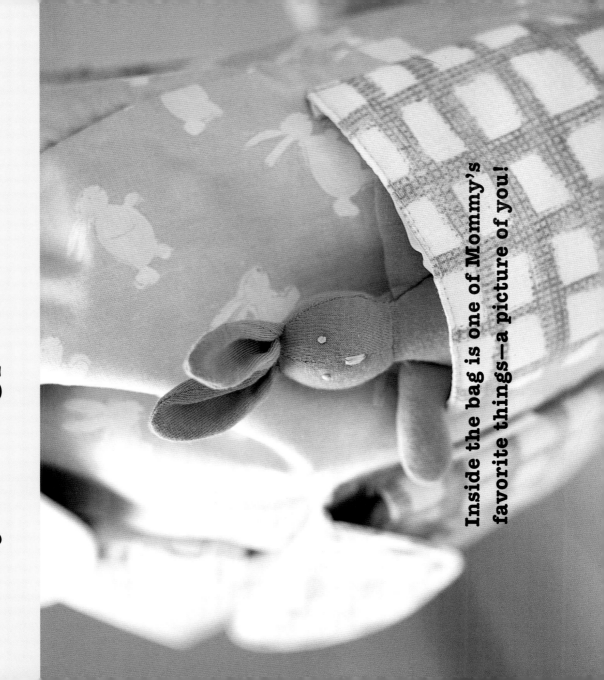

Mommy has a bag packed to take with her.

Inside the bag is one of Mommy's favorite things—a picture of you!

hospital is a safe place.

Nurses and doctors work at the hospital.

Nurses and doctors know how to help babies be born.

_____ will stay at the
hospital with Mommy.

_____ will give Mommy
water to drink, rub her back,
and hold her hand.

attach child's
photo here.

**Mommy will look at your picture
and that will make her happy!**

You will not be alone.

You and Mommy talked about

_____

who will take care of you.

**You will have lots of
fun together!**

You can play with your

_____

and _____ .

Draw a picture of your favorite toy.

When our baby
gives a big push,

Doctor _____
will help our baby be born.

You will have a big surprise!

Maybe you will have a brother.

Maybe you will have a sister.

Draw a picture of our new baby.

Our baby and Mommy will be tired.

will bring you to
the hospital to visit
baby and me.

We will stay in
the hospital for
a day or two.

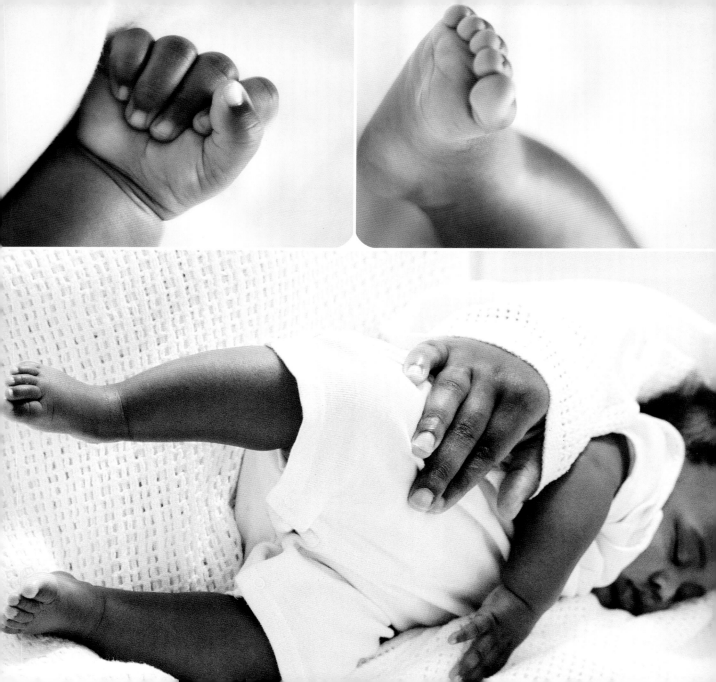

Our new baby

attach baby's
first photo
here

Welcome, baby!

The day our baby is born is called its birth day.

People will celebrate our baby's birth.

They will give our baby gifts.

Some of the gifts may be toys.

You can show our baby how to play.

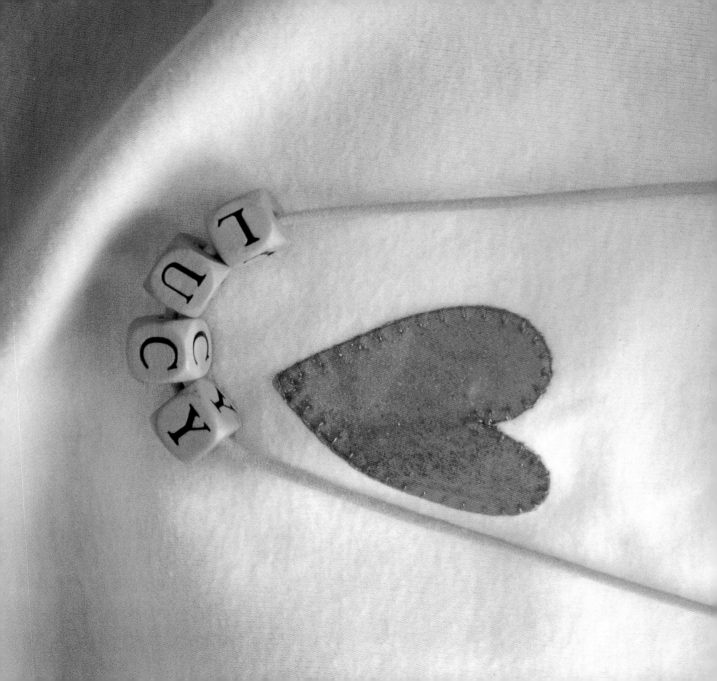

We will give our baby a name.

Maybe we will call our baby

_____ or _____ .

What do you think is a good name for our baby?

Let's call our baby

_____

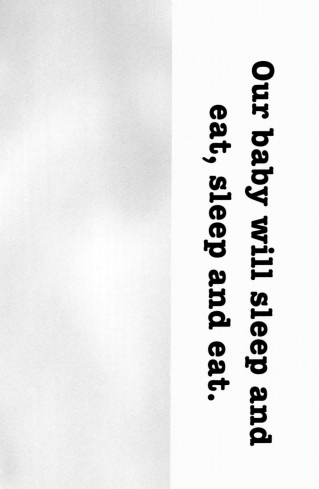

Our baby will sleep and eat, sleep and eat.

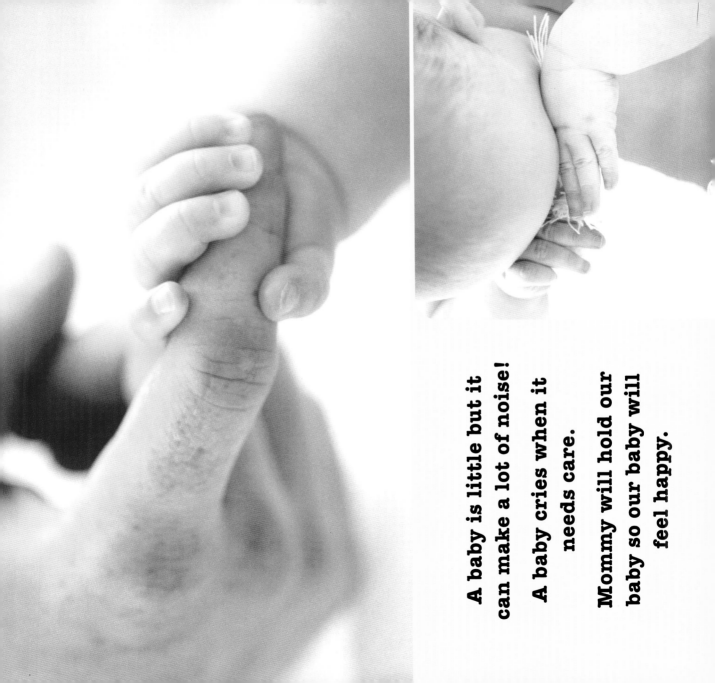

A baby is little but it can make a lot of noise!

A baby cries when it needs care.

Mommy will hold our baby so our baby will feel happy.

attach photo
of child and
baby here

Our baby and me

One day our baby will look at you and smile.

Credits and Acknowledgments

All photography by Debi Treloar, except page 38 by Lena Ikse-Bergman, and front cover & spine, pages 2, 10, 12, 14-15, 20–21, 23, 34, 44, 45 and 47 all © Stockbyte.